Microsoft PowerPoint 2016 N
A Step-by-Step Guide for F
By: Dr. Harold L. Fishe

MW00955562

Create Space Publishing
Seattle, Washington

ISBN: 13: 978-1530705894

Dedication

To my beautiful wife, Kym, who has always taught me to think outside the box and has been my strong support system every step of the way.

To my exceptional children, Brittani, Nicholas, and Sydnee: For the endurance, patience, encouragement, and love they have shown when daddy's hands were glued to the computer.

To my mom Johnetta Goodloe and my other mom Bonnie Hopkins, for their inspiration and guidance.

To my dad, who taught my about life on the golf course and during several fishing trips.

To my sisters Debra and Sheryl. I will always feel like I am trying to catch up with them.

To my heavenly Father: Without his calling in my life, this journey would not be possible to complete.

Finally, thanks to all of my students, friends and colleagues at College of Biblical Studies and Lone Star College who encouraged me to complete this project.

Preface

Since I was a child I was always fascinated with technology. I recall my first transistor radio and wondering "what makes this thing tick?" How does it work? Thus, I opened it up, took it apart and tried to wrap my feeble mind around what was far beyond my understanding. I have rubbed shoulders with some of the best IT guys in the field of technology over the years that helped to shape my ongoing hunger and thirst to understand technology. Although I have taken several technology courses in my life, I would say I have learned more through my hands-on experiences.

This book was developed through the heartfelt cries of my students over the years. Initially, students began to ask for my step-by-step instructional notes. Still other students would ask for both step-by-step notes along with pictures. After accumulating several notes over the years, I decided to publish my first two books, "A Technology Workbook for Christian Learners: Introduction to Microsoft Office 2010," and "A Technology Workbook for Adult Learners: Introduction to Microsoft Office 2010. However, this new book breaks down the content of Microsoft PowerPoint 2016 into smaller chunks of information. Chunking is an instructional strategy that involves breaking down information into "bite-sized" pieces so the brain can easily digest new information. Our working memory can only hold limited amounts of information at one time. This explains why each chapter in this book is much shorter, and will help to increase the retention of knowledge and skills that you will develop as you progress through the content.

Introduction

Microsoft (MS) PowerPoint was first released May 22, 1990 and has evolved over the years. MS PowerPoint is used for creating presentations for PC and Mac, and is a part of the Microsoft Office suite of production software. Microsoft PowerPoint is an excellent software program to learn, and some of the skills that are learned in this program can also apply to other software programs.

Job opportunities tend to pass some people by every day because they lack Microsoft Office skills today's employers are looking for. One of the most basic skills needed on any job is the creation of presentations using Microsoft PowerPoint. Research shows that Microsoft Office is the only software package ranked in the top 20 skills needed across all occupations. This means you become more marketable when you develop your skills in Microsoft PowerPoint.

Although this book is strategically designed for any individual who desires to have a basic understanding of Microsoft PowerPoint 2016, it can also benefit those who want to build on their prior knowledge. The overall goal of this user-friendly book is to develop the knowledge and skills that can be used at home and in the workplace. Although this is not an exhaustive book, it covers most of the commands found in Microsoft PowerPoint 2016.

Keep in mind that as you read this book there are multiple ways of completing a task in Microsoft PowerPoint. You will learn various techniques of modifying the appearance of slide backgrounds, formatting text, working with bullets, inserting pictures, using animations, slide transition, speaker notes, layouts, rehearsing slide shows, and much more. At the end of each chapter there are little known computer facts, applying knowledge and skills, and assessments along with the answers to each assessment question. Ultimately, at the completion of this book you will be able to confidently apply what you have learned from this book at home or on the job. Video tutorials are available under the same name at udemy.com. The digital form of this book is also available at redshelf.com.

Table of Contents

Chapter 1: Microsoft PowerPoint 2016 Introduction to PowerPoint

✓ Understanding PowerPoint
✓ Quick access toolbar
✓ Locating presentations

✓ Creating a simple presentation
✓ Previewing a presentation
✓ Saving a presentation

Understanding PowerPoint

What exactly is Microsoft (MS) PowerPoint? PowerPoint was designed for the creation of presentations with slides that contain text, pictures, movies, and other similar objects. A PowerPoint presentation can be viewed on video projectors, handouts, and directly on computers. Observe the various parts of PowerPoint below.

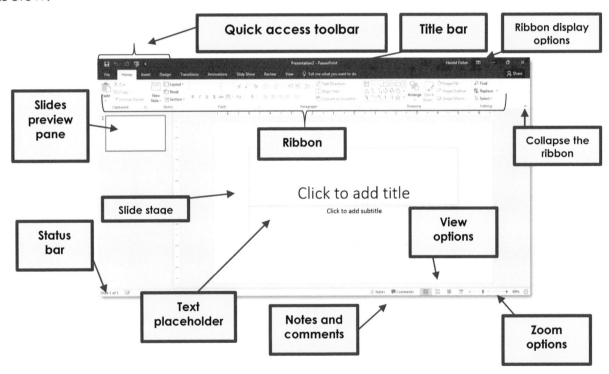

1. **Notice** the ribbon **tabs** found at the top of MS PowerPoint 2016.

2. The tabs are similar to those found in MS PowerPoint 2007, 2010 and 2013. Therefore, if you are familiar with previous versions of MS PowerPoint, you should not have a problem navigating around PowerPoint 2016.

In the upcoming chapters we will walk through most of the basic parts of these tabs. Each tab includes different command groups.

3. The **file** tab provides a backstage view of managing files and settings.
4. The **home** tab provides access to common commands, which includes the clipboard, slides, font, paragraph, drawing, and editing commands.
5. The **insert** tab allows us to insert various slide layouts, images, illustrations, add-ins, links, comments, text, symbols, and media commands.
6. The **design** tab provides themes to change and customize the background.
7. The **transitions** tab contains options that will allow you to change the effect and timing that occurs when you move from one slide to another in the slide show mode.
8. The **animations** tab allows you to change the timing of the movement of the text, images, and objects within your slides.
9. The **slide show** tab allows you to set up the way you want to display your presentation to an audience.
10. The **review** tab includes proofing, insights, language, comments, and comparing commands.
11. The **view** tab contains presentation views, master views, show, zoom, color/grayscale, window, and macro commands.
12. The **drawing tools format** tab will appear when a picture or object is selected. This tab includes insert shapes, shape styles, word art styles, arrange, and size commands.

13. The ribbon can be hidden. **Click** on the "**Ribbon Display option**" icon in the upper right-hand corner of your window.

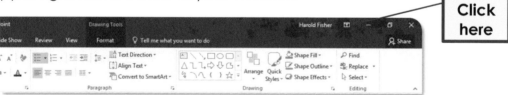

14. **Notice** the drop down menu options.

15. The first option allows you to hide the ribbon, which provides more working space within a document without any distractions.
16. The "Show tabs" option will only display the tabs on your ribbon.
17. The "Show tabs and Commands" is your defaulted view of the ribbon.
18. Make sure you are on the home tab.
19. **Leave** your presentation open for the next section.

Quick access toolbar

The quick access toolbar is a shortcut that allows the user to add just about any commonly used commands such as cut, copy, paste, and others to this toolbar for easy access. This toolbar can be moved below or above the ribbon and is found within Microsoft PowerPoint, Excel, Access, and Word 2016.

1. **Locate** your quick access toolbar, which is normally defaulted above the ribbon. (**Note**: It can be below your ribbon as well)

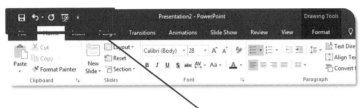

2. **Click** the down **arrow** at the end of your quick access toolbar and notice the options within the dropdown menu.

3. **Notice** the checked commands that are already found on your quick access toolbar.

4. If you click on any of the items checked, this will remove that command from the quick access toolbar.

5. **Click** on "**New**" and notice MS PowerPoint will add the "New" command to your quick access toolbar. (**Note**: "New" means adding a "new blank presentation").

Basically, this is a quicker way to open a new presentation instead of clicking file, then clicking new.

6. **Click** on "**More Commands.**"
7. **Notice** the are popular commands listed in the left column.
8. You can add each one by simply double-clicking or clicking on one and clicking the "add" button in the middle to move it over to the right column.

9. If you click the drop-down arrow and click "**All commands**" you will see all of the commands listed within Microsoft PowerPoint 2016 in the left column.

10. Once again, you can customize your quick access toolbar by adding any of these commands to the right column.

11. **Click** the "**cancel**" button in the bottom right-hand corner of this window.

12. **Click** the "**down arrow**" at the end of your quick access toolbar.

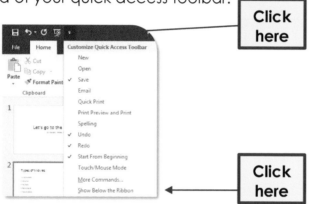

13. In the drop-down menu **click "Show Below the Ribbon."**

14. **Notice** your quick access toolbar is now below the ribbon.

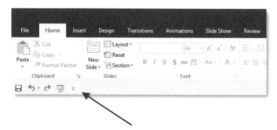

15. **Click** the **down arrow** again, and select "**Show above the Ribbon.**"

16. The quick access toolbar will move to its defaulted location above the ribbon.

17. **Keep** the presentation open for the next section.

Locating documents

1. For Windows 7 and 10 click on your "Windows Explorer" icon, which is normally located on your taskbar at the bottom of your desktop, or in the start menu by clicking on "computer", or located on your desktop. (This option will help only if you know the name of your document).

2. For Windows 8 users when you are on your desktop press the Ctrl Esc keys and start typing the name of your document in the search box, located in the upper right-hand corner of the window.

3. For Windows 7 and 10 users after clicking on the Windows Explorer icon type the name of the document in the **search box** located in the upper right-hand corner of the window.

4. In the event you don't know the name that was assigned to the document, open MS PowerPoint.
5. **Click** on the "File" tab. You should see the most recent documents listed underneath "options."
6. Notice the most recent documents listed.
7. In the event you do not see any of your recent documents, click on "**Options.**"

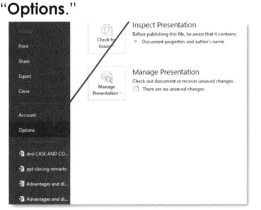 

8. When the PowerPoint options menu opens click on "**Advanced.**"

9. **Scroll** down to display. **Check** the box next to "**Quickly access this number of documents.**"

10. **Click** the **OK** button in the bottom right-hand corner when you are done.

Note: You can change the number of documents to be displayed.

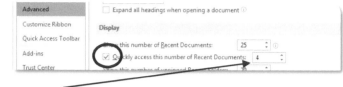

Creating a simple presentation

1. **Locate** Microsoft PowerPoint 2016 on your computer by **clicking** the "**Start button**" on the bottom left-hand side of your window. (**Note**: this will depend on the Windows operating system you have, Windows 7, 8, or 10).

2. **Notice** the example the right for locating Microsoft PowerPoint 2016 on a computer with Windows 7.

   However, if it is not found in your start menu, click "**All programs**" to locate it.

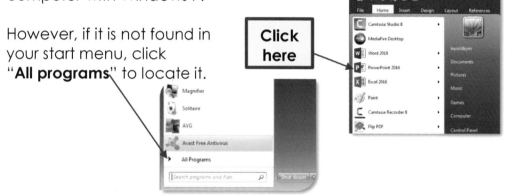

3. **Click on** MS PowerPoint 2016.
4. When MS PowerPoint opens, click on the "**blank presentation**" option.

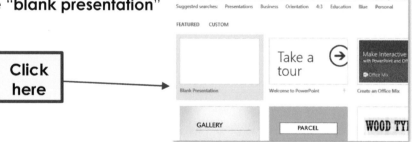

5. A blank presentation will open.

Note: From this point forward when you are asked to click, it will always be "left-clicking" your mouse unless otherwise directed to right-click.

6. **Notice** that when you open PowerPoint it opened to title slide layout, which is by default. This means the placeholders or text boxes that you see on this slide are designed for a title or cover page.

7. The top box states "Click to add title," while the bottom box is designed for a subtitle.

8. **Click** in the top box and type the following information: "**Let's Go to the Movies**."

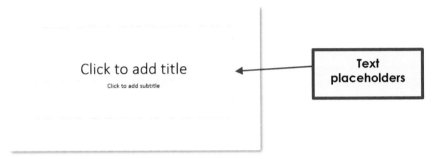

9. **Click** in the box below that says "Click to add subtitle" and type your name.

10. Your title slide should now look like this:

11. **Click** the "**New Slide**" icon on your ribbon.

Note: There are two parts to the new slide icon. The top part of the icon will simply add a new slide with the "Title and Content" layout. The bottom part of this icon will allow you to select the type of layout for the new slide that will be added.

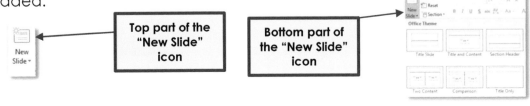

12. You should now have a second slide.
13. **Click** in the top placeholder that says "Click to add title"
14. **Type:** Types of Movies
15. **Click** in the placeholder below the title that says, "Click to add text."
16. **Type:** Comedies
17. **Press** the enter key on your keyboard (Notice bullets automatically appear).
18. **Type:** Drama
19. **Continue to press enter after you type the following words:**
20. Action, Romance, Animation.
21. Your slide should now look like the following:

22. Keep the presentation open for the next section.

Previewing a presentation

1. The presentation created in the last section should still be open.
2. There are three ways to view a presentation:
   a. **Click** on the Slide Show tab and select an option (From beginning or from current slide).

   b. **Press** the F5 key at the top of your keyboard. This takes you to the beginning of the presentation.
   c. **Click** on the "**Slide show**" icon located on the bottom right-hand side of your PowerPoint window.
3. **Click** on the "Slide Show" icon located on the bottom right-hand side of your window.

   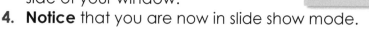
   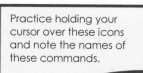

4. **Notice** that you are now in slide show mode.
5. If you want to exit from slide show you can either press your space bar or press your escape (Esc) key located on the upper left-hand corner of your PowerPoint window.

Practice holding your cursor over these icons and note the names of these commands.

6. **Click** on slide one in the navigation pane on the left
Side of your PowerPoint window and you will be on the first slide of your presentation.
7. **Keep** the document open for the next section.

Saving a presentation

1. **Open** the PowerPoint presentation from the last section.
2. **Click** on the "file" tab.
3. **Click** on "save-as."

Note: It does not matter at this point if you clicked on "save" or "save-as" because either way the "save-as" window will appear.

4. **Click** "Browse"
5. A window will open.
6. **Type** the name "My First Presentation" and **save** it to your desktop like the example on the next page.

7. **Look** on your desktop and notice the presentation is now saved. The next time you want to open it, simply double-click on this file and it will open.
8. **Close** the presentation by clicking on the **X** in the upper right-hand corner of your PowerPoint software window.

Chapter 1: Glossary

Placeholder: The placeholders are the dotted borders of text boxes found within different slide layouts. They help to guide the users in the placement of titles and bullet points.

Ribbon: This is the menu bar and tabs located at the top of your PowerPoint software. It contains several different commands used to create a presentation.

Slide show: A slide show is a collection of slides arranged in a certain order that contain text, images, and objects for presenting before an audience.

Chapter 1: Applying your skills

1. **Open** PowerPoint to a new blank document.
2. **Type** "My First Presentation in the title of your first slide and add a new slide.
3. **Preview** the presentation in "Slide show" mode.
4. **Save** the presentation as "My second presentation to your desktop.

Chapter 1: Self-Assessment

1. **True or False:** Microsoft PowerPoint was originally designed for justifying text only.
2. **Locating** Microsoft PowerPoint 2016 on your computer will depend on what factor? **A.** Screen resolution, **B.** Operating system, **C.** Desktop organization
3. **Which** of the following is not a view option: **A.** Web layout, **B.** Draft, **C.** Read layout
4. **True or False:** There are at least five different ways to enter the slide show mode in MS PowerPoint 2016.
5. **True or False:** When you save a presentation you need to name it and provide a location where it will be saved.

Answers:

1. False (MS PowerPoint was designed for designing presentation)
2. Operating system (Win 7, 8, or 10)
3. C. Read layout
4. False (There are three ways)
5. True

Chapter 2: Microsoft PowerPoint 2016 Views, Layouts, and Formatting Text

✓ Changing views
✓ Adding layouts

✓ Formatting text
✓ Formatting bullets

Changing views

Let's experiment with changing the various presentation views found in MS PowerPoint.

1. **Open** the presentation from the last chapter.
2. **Click** on the "**view**" tab on your ribbon at the top.

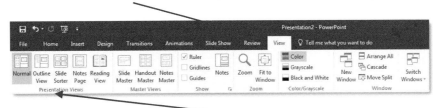

3. **Notice** the five options on the "<u>views</u>" menu of your ribbon. (There are master and slide show views as well)

   Note: Each view will help you manage and view a presentation in various ways. Also, read mode, print layout, and web layout are found on the bottom right side of the MS PowerPoint window.
   ✓ **Normal view**: This view is the defaulted view in PowerPoint 2016, which includes slide and notes panes.
   ✓ **Outline view**: This view focuses on the content of your presentation. It is used to adjust the structure of text.
   ✓ **Slide Sorter**: This view displays all of the slides so that you can change their order.
   ✓ **Notes Page**: This view displays the speaker notes you will use for your presentation.
   ✓ **Reading view**: This view displays the presentation in a window, which makes it easy to review.
   ✓ **Slide Show view**: This is the view you will be using to display your presentation before an audience.

4. At the moment, you are in the defaulted "Normal" view. (Notice this view is highlighted).
5. **Click** on the "**Outline**" view and notice the change in how the presentation is displayed.

6. Repeat the previous action with the slide sorter, notes page, and reading views.
7. **Click** the "**Normal**" view again to return to your defaulted view.
8. **Keep** the document open for the next section.

Adding layouts

1. This section provides a quick review of what you learned about layouts in chapter one.
2. You should still have the presentation open from the last section.
3. Make sure you are on the home tab of the ribbon.
4. **Click** on slide 2 in the slide window of your presentation.

5. **Click** on the top part of the "New Slide" icon.
6. You should now have three slides.
7. You learned in chapter 1 that if you clicked the bottom part of the "New Slide" icon, then you have the option to change the slide layout.
8. You can also change the slide layout of an existing slide.

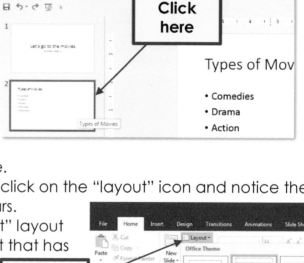

9. Since you are now on slide 3, click on the "layout" icon and notice the drop-down menu that appears.
10. **Notice** that "Title and Content" layout is highlighted. This is the layout that has been applied to this slide.
11. **Click** on the "Comparison" layout.
12. **Notice** that the comparison layout has been applied to slide three.
13. If you add another slide, this same layout will be applied until you change the layout.
14. Keep your presentation open for the next section.

Formatting text

1. You should still have the presentation open from the last section.
2. **Click** on slide two.
3. In order to change the formatting of your words, they need to be highlighted first.

4. For example, highlight all of your bullets. (**Note**: PowerPoint will not allow you to highlight the bullet. Therefore, place your cursor in front of the first word to highlight).

5. Now you can use your formatting tools on your home tab to change the font style, font size, font color, etc.

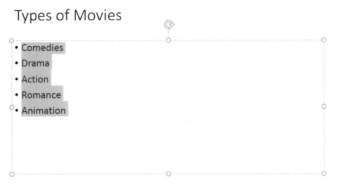

6. **Click** the "Bold" icon. Notice your text is now bold.
7. **Click** bold again and notice the bold formatting is removed.

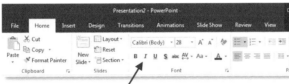

8. **Click** the italic icon. Notice your text is now italicized.
9. **Click** the italic icon again and the italic formatting is removed.
10. **Repeat** the same steps above for the underline and text shadow icons.

11. You can also change the font type by clicking on the down arrow in the font window.
12. **Notice** that the font list is in alphabetical order.
13. **Locate** "Times New Roman" and **click** on it.
14. Your text should now be "Times New Roman."
15. You can also change the size of your text by clicking on the down arrow in the icon to the right of the font style. (**Note**: Your text should still be highlighted).

16. **Click** the down arrow for the font size and change it to 40 pts.

   Note: The font size should be a least 28 pts. If you made your fonts smaller your audience will have a difficult time viewing your presentation clearly.

17. **Click** the font size down arrow again and change the size to 28 pts.

18. **Notice** the two icons to the right of the font size icon.

19. **Hold** your cursor over them and notice that one icon will increase the font size and the other one will decrease the font size.

20. If you wanted to cut and paste your bullets to another slide your text should be highlighted to perform these commands. (**Note**: The cut command will move text, pictures, and objects to a different location).

21. **Highlight** the first bullet and click on the "cut" icon.

22. **Notice** the first bullet disappears.

23. **Click** at the end of the last bullet and press the enter key on your keyboard.

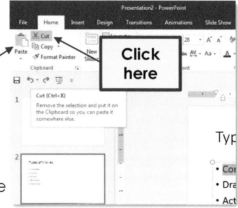

24. **Click** on the "Paste" icon and notice the first bullet is now at the bottom.

25. The same steps above work for the copy command. However, the copy command is simply designed to place a second copy of the same text, object, or pictures that you copied.

26. Keep your presentation open for the next section.

Formatting bullets

1. You should still have the presentation open from the last section.
Note: The purpose of bullets is to make a key point. Bullets are used in MS Word as well as MS PowerPoint.
2. Your bullets on slide two should still be highlighted.
3. **Click** on the **drop-down arrow** of the bullet icon and notice the various options you have for changing your bullets.
4. **Move** your cursor over any of the other bullet options within the gallery and notice the preview of how the bullets will look.
5. **Click** one of these options.
6. Keep in mind the same options apply to the numbering icon located to the right of the bullet icon.
7. **Save** and **close** the presentation.

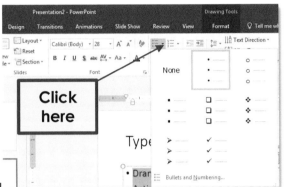

Chapter 2: Glossary

Slide show view: This is the view you will be using to display your presentation before an audience.

Cut command: The cut command will move text, pictures, and objects to a different location.

Bullets: The purpose of bullets is to make key points. Bullets are used in MS Word as well as MS PowerPoint.

Chapter 2: Applying your skills

1. **Open** Microsoft PowerPoint 2016 to a new blank document.
2. **Add** a new slide and **change** your view to slide sorter.
3. **Change** back to the normal view and change the layout to "Two Content."
4. **Type** the following as a title on slide two: "Computers".
5. **Type** two bullet points: Mouse and Monitor.
6. **Close** the document without saving it.

Chapter 2: Self-Assessment

1. **True or False:** PowerPoint should be in the reading view when you present before an audience.
2. **True or False**: Layouts can be changed when you add a new slide or after you have added a new slide.
3. **True or False:** You do not have to highlight your bulleted text in order to make changes.
4. **True or False:** Bullets can be changed by selecting the down arrow on the bullets icon.
5. **True or False:** Applying numbers to your bulleted list can be performed by simply clicking on the font icon.

Answers:

1. False (PowerPoint should be in the "Slide Show" view when you present before an audience).
2. True
3. False (Actually, you do need to highlight the text in order to format it)
4. True
5. False (Click on the numbering icon to change your bullets to numbers).

Chapter 3: Microsoft PowerPoint 2016 Speaker Notes, Pictures, and Sound

✓ Speaker notes
✓ Adding pictures
✓ Using gridlines

✓ Inserting sound
✓ Undo and re-do commands

Speaker notes

The purpose of speaker notes is for you to use as a reference while you are presenting your PowerPoint presentation to an audience. You can print out your speaker notes and have them on the podium as you are speaking.

1. **Open** you MS PowerPoint presentation you created in chapter one.
2. **Click** on slide 2 of your presentation.
3. **Notice** the "Notes" icon at the bottom of your presentation window.
4. **Click** on the "Notes" icon.

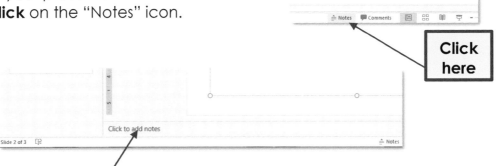

5. The notes window will open near the bottom of your presentation.
6. **Click** on top of "Click to add notes" and type: Elaborate on the different genres of movies today.
7. You can also add and edit your speaker notes found under the view tab.
8. **Click** on the view tab, then **click** the "Notes page" icon.
9. **Notice** the notes page with the notes you just added to this slide.
10. Keep in mind you can still add more notes to this slide (and others), edit, and print these notes when you present.
11. **Change** your view to Normal.
12. **Click** the "save" icon on your quick access toolbar.

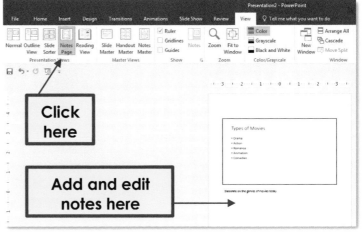

13. **Keep** the presentation open for the next section.

Adding pictures

1. **Open** the presentation from the last section.
2. **Click** on slide 2 of your presentation.

   Note: In order to insert a picture within your presentation you can simply go to a license free website like pixabay.com, copy and paste the picture into your slide. You can also insert a picture that was saved to your computer by clicking on the insert tab and the picture icon.

3. **Open** an internet browser and navigate to www.pixabay.com.
4. **Type** "Movie Theater" in the search box.
5. **Locate** the following image, copy and paste it into slide two.
6. **Resize** the picture by moving your cursor over any corner and you will see a double-sided arrow.
7. **Click**, hold, and drag towards the center of the picture in order to make the picture smaller.
8. **Place** the picture on the right side of your bullets.
9. Your presentation should look like the example to the right.
10. You can also flip a picture so the character in the picture is faced in a different direction.
11. **Click** on your picture so that it is selected.
12. Move your cursor over the middle dot on the right side of the picture.

Types of Movies

• Drama
• Action
• Romance
• Animation
• Comedies

13. When you see a double-sided arrow, click/hold and drag to the left until the character in the picture is facing towards the left.
14. **Open** your browser again and locate www.pixabay.com.
15. In the search box type: Movie reel.
16. **Click** on the following picture.

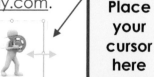

Place your cursor here

17. **Look** for the download button on the right-hand side of the page and click on it.
18. **Select** the option M – 1280 X 1280.
19. **Click** "download" and the following window will appear. ⟶
20. **Click** "OK."

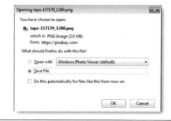

21. **Click** the "insert" tab.
22. **Click** on the "Pictures" icon.
23. **Click** on "downloads."
24. **Click** on the picture of the reel.
25. **Click** on "insert."
26. The picture is now on slide two. You may need to resize the picture.

Note: You can also insert pictures through the "Online Pictures" icon as well.

27. Slide two should look like the following example.
28. **Keep** the presentation open for the next section.

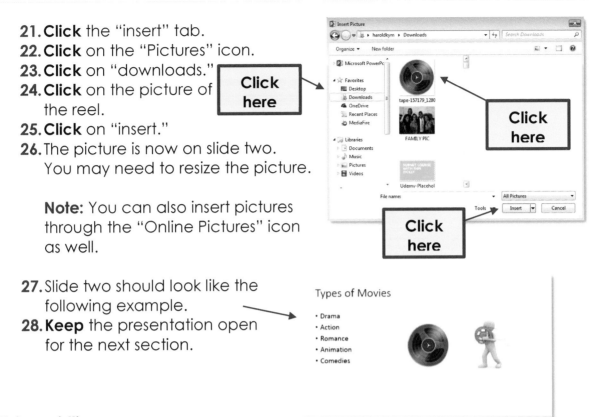

Using gridlines

The gridlines help you to align your pictures and objects on a slide.

1. **Open** the presentation from the previous section.
2. **Click** on slide two.
3. **Click** on the "View" tab on your ribbon.
4. **Click** in the empty box next to "Gridlines" and your gridlines will be visible within your slide.

5. **Move** your pictures even with the horizontal gridline just above the bullet "acition.

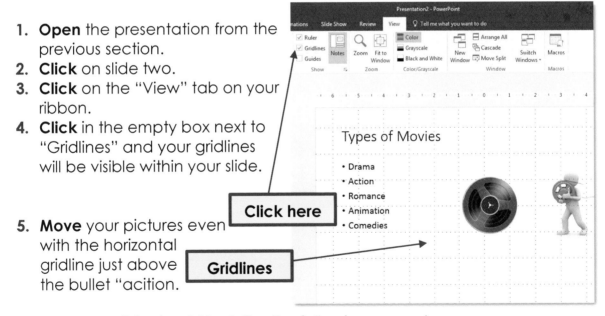

6. Now your slide should look like the following example.
7. **Save** the presentation for the next section.

Inserting sound

1. You should still have the presentation open from the previous section.
2. **Click** on slide two of your presentation.
3. **Click** on the insert tab.
4. **Look** for the "audio" icon on the right-hand side of your ribbon.
5. **Click** on the audio icon and notice the two options, "Audio on My PC," and "Record Audio."
6. If you had previously recorded audio saved to your PC, then you click on "Audio on My PC."
7. **Open** your internet browser and navigate to www.brainybetty.com.
8. **Look** on the left-hand side of the website and **click** on "Music for Presentations."
9. **Click** on the "Hi-Tech" link.
10. A window will open. **Click** "save file" then **click** "OK."
11. **Go** back to your PowerPoint presentation.
12. **Make** sure you are on the insert tab.
13. **Click** the audio icon and **click** "Audio on My PC."
14. **Search** for "downloads" and click on it. **Note:** This demonstration is for Windows 7).
15. Locate the "HiTech" file and double-click on it.
16. The file will be placed within slide two.
17. **Notice** the speaker that appears on the slide.
18. **Click** the forward arrow (play button) to hear the sound. (If you don't see the play button move your cursor over the speaker).
19. **Click** on the speaker and notice the "audio tools" tab that automatically appears on your ribbon.
20. Click on the "playback" tab.
21. Notice the options.
22. If you wanted the audio to play automatically when you are in slide show, you would click the down arrow next to "start" and select "automatically."
23. If you want the audio to play across all the slides, check the box next to "Play across Slides."

Notice the two options here

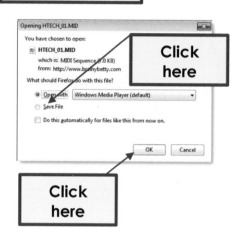

Click here

Click here

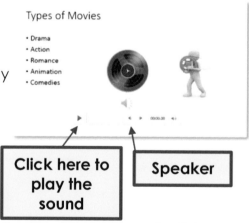

Click here to play the sound

Speaker

24. You could also check "Loop until Stopped" so that the music will play continuously until you stop it.
25. Make sure your "start" is set at "automatically."
26. **Click** the "Slide show" icon on the bottom right-hand side of your presentation and the audio should start playing.
27. **Press** the Esc (escape) key on your keyboard.

If you wanted to record audio and save it to your presentation, you would select "Record Audio." (In order to record you will need a microphone. Most laptops have built-in-microphones).

Note: You will learn how to add voice-over (audio) to a presentation in chapter ten.

28. **Keep** the presentation open for the next section.

Undo and redo commands

The undo command will reverse the previous actions performed in a document or multiple actions that occurred previously. The redo command will repeat the last action. However, once you save and close a document you cannot undo or redo previous actions when you open the document again. **Note**: Some actions can't be undone. If you can't undo an action, the undo command button changes to "Can't Undo."

1. You should still have the presentation open from the last section.
2. In the navigation window on the left-hand side where you have three slides, click on slide three.
3. **Press** your delete key on your keyboard and slide 3 will be removed.
4. **Click** the undo button and notice slide 3 will appear again.

5. This also works for any other action performed in PowerPoint since it has been opened.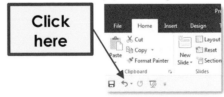

6. **Click** the "**redo**" command and notice the slide three is removed again.
7. **Save and close** the presentation.

Chapter 3: Glossary

Speaker notes: The purpose of speaker notes is for you to use as a reference while you are presenting your PowerPoint presentation to an audience.

Gridlines: Gridlines help you to align your pictures and objects on a slide.

Undo and re-do: The undo command will reverse the previous actions performed in a document or multiple actions that occurred previously. The redo command will repeat the last action. However, once you save and close a document you cannot undo or redo previous actions when you open the document again.

Chapter 3: Applying your skills

1. **Open** Microsoft PowerPoint 2016 to a new blank presentation.
2. **Open** speaker notes and add "Introduce yourself" at the bottom of the first slide.
3. **Add** a second slide and add any random picture from pixabay.com.
4. **Turn** the gridlines on.
5. **Type** "Understanding Routers" as a title at the top of slide two and click the undo command.

Chapter 3: Self-Assessment

1. **True or False:** You can create speaker notes for your presentation, however you will be unable to print them out.
2. **True or False**: Pictures can be flipped so that the character within a picture is facing a different direction.
3. **True or False:** Gridlines help to paste pictures within a slide.
4. **True or False:** There are two options for inserting sound, "Audio on My PC," and "Record Audio."

Answers:

1. False (You can print out your speaker notes)
2. True
3. False (Gridlines help you to align pictures on a slide)
4. True

Chapter 4: Microsoft PowerPoint 2016 Animation, Backgrounds, & Templates

- ✓ Working with animation
- ✓ Advanced animation
- ✓ Design themes
- ✓ Formatting backgrounds

Working with animation

An animation effect sets up the way you want text, picture, or an object to appear on your slide during a slide show presentation. You can set text to appear by the letter, word, or paragraph. There are four categories of animation, which includes entrance, emphasis, exit, and motion paths.

1. **Open** the presentation from the previous chapter and make sure you are on slide two.
2. **Click** inside the placeholder where your bullets are located.
3. **Click** the animation tab on your ribbon.
4. **Click** on the **drop down arrow** to view more animations. Notice there are four options for applying animation to your text (or objects). However, focus on the animations under the heading "entrance."
5. **Click** on the "**Fly in**" option.
6. **Notice** the preview that PowerPoint provided when you selected the "Fly in" animation.
7. Also, **notice** the numbers that appear next to each of the bullets. They are 1-5, meaning this is the order that your bullets will appear on the slide.
8. **Click** on the "preview" icon on the left side of your ribbon to see the animation again.

9. **Click** on the "**Slide Show**" tab, and then click "**From Beginning**."

10. **You will be on slide one. Press** your space bar and notice that you will move to slide two.

11. **Press** the space bar again and notice how your bullets will animate. Repeat the same steps for the rest of your bullets until all of them fly into the slide.

   Note: In the event you press the spacebar to many times and pass up your intended bullet, simply hit the backspace button on your keyboard. There are multiple ways to cause your animation to occur in your presentation. You can press your spacebar, click the mouse, use your arrow keys, press enter, or use a remote device to advance from one animation to the next. This is also true when advancing from one slide to the next.

12. **Press** the "escape" (Esc) key located in the upper left-hand corner of your keyboard to exit the slide show.

13. **Keep** the presentation open for the next section.

Advanced animation

In this section you will learn how to add a second animation so that each bullet point will appear within the slide one by one in the slide show mode.

1. **Open** the presentation from the previous chapter and make sure you are on slide two.
2. **Click** on the "animations" tab.
3. **Click** inside the placeholder where your bullets are located.
4. **Click** on the "animation pane" icon.
5. **Notice** the animation pane that that opens on the right-hand side of your window.
6. The list of animated bullets will appear.
7. **Click** on the number 1, which is "**drama**" in the animation pane.
8. **Click** the "Add Animation" button, which is located on the "advanced animation" section of your ribbon.
9. **Scroll** down in the drop down window until you locate "Fly out." **Click** on it.
10. At the bottom of the list in the animation pane you will see a double arrow. **Click** on it.
11. **Notice** there is a new list of animations for each of our bullet points.

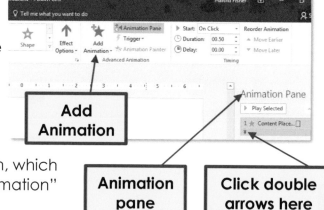

12. **Click/hold/drag** number 6 to the second position in the list. (Notice the line that appears as you drag number six. This line will help you place it in the correct position).

13. You should now have two dramas at the beginning of your list. However, the first drama has the "fly-in" animation applied to it, while the second one will "fly-out."

14. **Move** (click/hold/drag) "action" up to the third position just below the first "action."

15. **Repeat** the previous actions until your animation pane looks like the following example below.

16. **Click** the "Slide Show" icon on the bottom right-hand side of your window to test the animation. Notice that each bullet will fly out and fly in one-by-one.

17. You can also change the timing of each animation so that when one animation disappears the next animation will appear.

18. **Click** on "Action" (3rd position) in the animation pane.

19. **Click** on the down arrow on the "Start" option (on the ribbon) and change it to "With previous." (This means "action" will appear when "drama" disappears).

20. **Click** on number 4 "Romance" in the navigation pane and change it to "With Previous."

21. **Click** on number 5 "Animation" and change it to "With Previous."

22. **Click** on number 7 "Comedies" and change it to "With Previous."

23. **Click** the "Slide Show" icon on the bottom right-hand side of your window to test the animation. Now each bullet will appear one by one followed by a new bullet appearing in the slide show.

24. **Close** the **"navigation pane** and **save** the presentation for the next section.

Design themes

Backgrounds should add a nice touch to your presentation and not distract from your bullet points. The most important thing to remember is that the audience should be able to see your text (bullet points) without any distractions in the background. If you find a background that you really like, but it seems difficult to find the right color text, then either you need to search for another background or tone down the chosen background. Therefore, make wise decisions!

1. **Open** the PowerPoint presentation from the previous section.

2. **Click** on the "Design" tab and simply move your cursor (slowly) over the various designs.
3. **Notice** how PowerPoint will provide a preview of each design on your slide.

4. **Click** the drop down menu in order to see more designs.

5. **Select** any of the available designs by simply clicking on it. Notice that each design will automatically change your background and text color as well. (Note: Some of these designs will reduce your text size below what is recommended, which is 28 font size. Therefore, you may need to adjust your text sizes for some of these designs).
6. **Keep** the presentation open for the next section.

Formatting backgrounds

1. **Click** the "Format Background" icon on the far right-hand side of your ribbon.
2. The "Format Background" navigation pane will open on the right-hand side. You can fill your background with a solid color, gradient, picture, texture or pattern.
3. **Click** the down arrow next to the "paint" bucket and select any color.
4. **Notice** the color is applied to the background of your slide.

5. If you decided to keep the color Then you would also click on "Apply To All" near the bottom of the navigation window.
6. **Notice** "Transparency" as well. Basically, transparency allows you to make the color brighter or darker.
7. **Click** "Gradient Fill" and notice the options.
8. Gradient fill allows you to select two different colors, and change the direction of the colors on the slide.
9. You will learn how to add a picture to your background in the next chapter.
10. **Click** on "pattern fill" and notice the options.

11. Remember, if you select any of these options click "**Apply to All**" so that any changes you make will be applied to all of your slide backgrounds.
12. **Close** the "format background" navigation window.
13. **Save** and close the presentation.

Chapter 4: Glossary

Animation: These are the effects that set up the way you want text, picture, or an object to appear on your slide during a slide show presentation.

Gradient fill: This option provides a gradual blending to two or more colors within a shape or the background of a slide.

Design themes: These options make it much easier to coordinate the colors of your background and text for your presentation. They are preformatted backgrounds that you can apply instead of manually changing the text colors and backgrounds.

Chapter 4: Applying your skills

1. **Open** Microsoft PowerPoint 2016 to a new blank presentation.
2. **Add** a second slide and type the words "Windows" as a bullet, and "Mac" as the second bullet.
3. **Add** the "float-in" animation to these bullet points.
4. **Change** the background of both slides to any design template.
5. **Close** the document without saving it.

Chapter 4: Self-Assessment

1. **True or False:** You must click inside the placeholder where your bullets are located before you can apply animation.
2. **True or False:** In order to apply a second animation to your bullets you must click on the "second animation" icon.
3. **True or False:** There are four different options to select in order to format your background.
4. **True or False:** If you want the same background on all of your slides you simply need to apply a design theme.
5. **True or False:** If you find a background that you really like, but it seems difficult to find the right color text, then either you need to search for another background or tone down the chosen background.

Answers:

1. True
2. False (Actually, it is called "Add Animation.")
3. True
4. False (You must use "Apply to All")
5. True

Chapter 5: Microsoft PowerPoint 2016
Slide Size and Transition

✓ Pictures as backgrounds
✓ Slide size

✓ Slide transition
✓ Transition timing

Pictures as backgrounds

Applying pictures to the background of a slide is an easy task. However, it is important to remember that the background of a slide should not stand out more than the color of your bullet points.

1. **Open** an internet browser (Google Chrome or Firefox) and go to www.pixabay.com.
2. **Type** "**Movie backgrounds**" in the search box and press the "enter" key on your keyboard.
3. Try to find the following image:

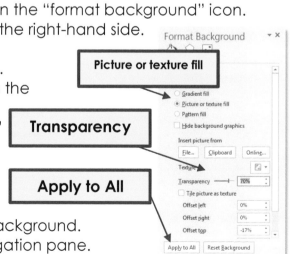

4. Once you find the image, **right-click** on the image and select "**save picture as**" or "**save image as**" in the drop-down menu. (Save it to your desktop).
5. **Open** your PowerPoint presentation from the last chapter.
6. **Click** on slide two.
7. **Click** on the "design" tab and **click** on the "format background" icon.
8. Your navigation window will open on the right-hand side.
9. **Click** on "Picture or texture fill."
10. **Click** on "File" and windows will open.
11. **Locate** your picture that you saved to the desktop.
12. **Click** on the picture and click "insert." (The picture will be inserted into the background of the slide).
13. **Change** your transparency to 70%.
14. **Click** "Apply to All."
15. All of your slides will have the same background.
16. **Close** the "format background" navigation pane.
17. **Save** the document and keep it open for the next section.

Slide size

Whenever you open PowerPoint and start building a presentation, your slide size is defaulted to 10 X 7.5 inches. However, you can change the size of your slides if necessary.

1. **Open** the MS PowerPoint 2016 you worked on in the last section.
2. **Click** on the "design" tab.
3. **Click** on the "slide size" icon.
4. **Notice** the options, standard or Widescreen.
5. **Click** on "Custom Slide Size."
6. At the moment your slides are defaulted to "Widescreen."
7. **Click** the down arrow next to "Widescreen" and notice there are more options.
   Note: We will use the "Banner" option in chapter six.
8. Other options include changing the width, height, and the number for each slide.
9. **Click** cancel and keep the presentation open for the next section.

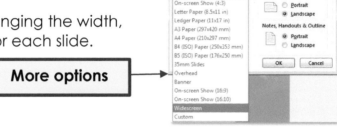

Slide transition

Slide transitions are visual movements that occur between slides. For example, when you move from one slide to the next, you can apply any type of slide transition. The key is to make sure you use the "Apply to All" option once you select your transition.

1. **Open** the MS PowerPoint 2016 presentation from the previous section.
2. **Click** on the "Transitions" tab, then click on the drop-down arrow to reveal more transition options.

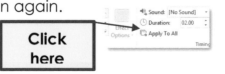

3. **Select** the "Push" transition from the list. (Notice when you select a transition, PowerPoint will provide a preview.
4. **Click** the "Preview" button in the upper left-hand corner in order to see the transition again.
5. **Click** the "Apply to All" button.
6. **Click** on the "Slide show" icon in the bottom right-hand corner of your window.

7. **Press** the space bar on your keyboard to advance your slides and notice the slide transition that was applied.
   Note: Keep in mind that you can change the transition to any other option.
8. **Save** the presentation and keep it open for the next section.

Transition timing

The timing of transition in your slide show depends on the task you want to accomplish. For example, you can determine the length of time the slide will be displayed before it moves to the next slide automatically. You can also set the amount of time the transition will take place when it happens. This means if you apply the push transition at ten seconds, this is the amount of time it will take for this transition to occur.

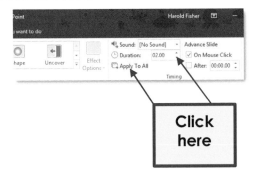

1. **Open** the presentation from the previous section.
2. **Click** on the "Transitions" tab.
3. **Notice** on the far right-hand side you can apply sound.
4. **Click** the "down-arrow" next to "Sound."
5. **Select** the "Camera" sound.
6. **Change** the duration to 01.25.
7. **Click** "Apply to All."

Note: In the last section you applied the "Push" transition. If you have not done this, click on "push" and then click "Apply to All" again.

8. **Click** "Preview" on the far left-hand side of the ribbon. (This will provide a quick preview of how the presentation will behave while in slide show).
9. **Notice** the "Advance Slide" section on the far right-hand side of your ribbon. At the moment "On Mouse Click" should have a check mark next to it. This means when you are in slide show you can manually advance the slides. However, you can change these settings so that PowerPoint will automatically advance the slides for you.
10. **Click** in the box next to "On Mouse Click" so that the check mark will disappear.
11. **Click** in the box next to "After" and **change** the timing to 00:00.05.
12. **Click** "Apply To All."
13. **Click** on the "Slide Show" tab.
14. **Click** "From Beginning."
15. **Notice** how fast the show moves.
16. You can adjust the timing to slow it Down by increasing the "Duration" and "After" timings.
17. **Save and close** the presentation.

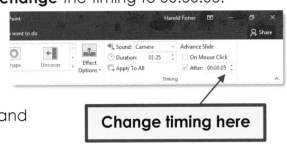

Chapter 5: Glossary

Transition: Slide transitions are visual movements that occur between slides. For example, when you move from one slide to the next, you can apply any type of slide transition

Transparency: This is the setting in PowerPoint that allows you to change a picture from a darker color to a brighter contrast.

Duration: The amount of time the transition will take place when your presentation advances to the next slide.

Chapter 5: Applying your skills

1. **Open** Microsoft PowerPoint 2016 to a new blank presentation.
2. **Type** the words "Technology geeks are awesome" on slide one and apply any "design" to the background.
3. **Add** a new slide and **apply** any slide transition.
4. **Change** the settings of slide transition to advance every ten seconds.
5. **Close** the presentation without saving it.

Chapter 5: Self-Assessment

1. **True or False:** If you add a picture in the background of the slides it will automatically appear on every slide in your presentation.
2. **True or False:** You can actually create a banner under the slide size settings.
3. **True or False:** Slide transition is the movement of the slides when you advance from one slide to another.
4. **True or False:** The duration is the overall timing of the slide transition.
5. **True or False:** Whenever you make changes to the timing section of transitions you should always click "Apply To All" if you want these timings applied to the entire slide show.

Answers:

1. False (You still need to click "Apply To All" whenever you add a picture in the background of your slides)
2. True
3. True
4. False (Duration is the amount of time the transition will take place when your presentation advances to the next slide)
5. True

Chapter 6: Microsoft PowerPoint 2016
Slide Master, Numbers, and Banners

✓ Sorting slides
✓ Editing slide master

✓ Inserting slide numbers
✓ Creating a banner

Sorting slides

Slides can be sorted within the slide navigation window on the left-hand side of your window or by clicking on the slide sorter icon found under the view tab.

1. **Open** the PowerPoint presentation from the last chapter.
2. Click on the "Slide Sorter" icon located on the bottom right-hand side of your window.

Slide Sorter icons

3. Your presentation should now be in the slide sorter view like the following example to the right.
4. **Notice** that you were automatically moved to the view tab.
5. Also, notice the other "Slide Sorter" icon on the ribbon, which is found under the view tab.
6. **Click/hold/drag** slide 1 to the right of slide two. Notice that you can reverse the order of your slides. You can also delete a slide by simply clicking on it and pressing the delete button on your keyboard. (Note: you can also perform these same actions in the normal view)
7. **Click/hold/drag** on slide 2 and drag it back to the left of slide now. This slide sorter option is very beneficial when you have multiple slides.
8. **Click** on the "Normal" icon and you will be taken back to the previous view.
9. **Keep** the presentation open for the next section.

Editing slide master

The slide master view allows you to control the look of your PowerPoint presentations. This means you can change the colors, fonts, backgrounds, along with anything else on all of your slides in one step instead of modifying individual slides.

1. **Open** the MS PowerPoint presentation from the last section.
2. **Click** on the "view" tab.
3. **Click** on the "Slide Master" icon.
4. Since you are on slide one, the slide master will display the same layout used on slide one. Any formatting changes you make for your fonts will also be applied to the entire presentation.
5. **Notice** the options of changing themes, colors, fonts, effects, background styles, etc.
6. **Click** on the "Themes" icon and note the options to change to a different theme in the drop down menu.
7. **Click** the "Slice" theme and notice the change that is made to the entire presentation
8. **Click** the undo icon.
9. **Click** the fonts icon.
10. **Select** "Franklin Gothic."
11. **Look** on the far right-hand side of your ribbon and **click** the "Close Master View" icon.
12. **Notice** that all of your fonts are now Franklin Gothic.
13. **Save** and keep the presentation open for the next section.

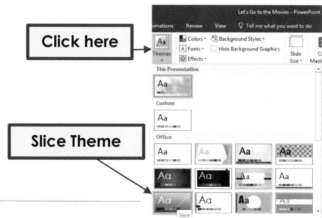

Click here

Slice Theme

Inserting slide numbers

Slide numbers can help you as the speaker keep track of the correct slide that is being displayed that should correspond with your personal notes as well as the handouts you provide for your audience.

1. **Open** PowerPoint presentation from the last section.
2. **Click** on the insert tab and notice the "Slide number" icon on the right-hand side of the ribbon.
3. **Click** on the slide number icon and the header/footer window will open.
4. **Click** in the box next to "Slide number"
5. **Click** "Apply To All."
6. **Look** in the bottom right-hand corner of

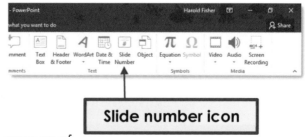

Slide number icon

your slides and notice the slide number has been applied.
7. **Save** and keep the presentation open for the next section.

Creating a banner

Banners can be used for specific events, titles, headings, or online course banners in Blackboard.

1. **Open** Microsoft PowerPoint to a new blank document.
2. **Click** on the design tab.
3. **Click** on the "Slide size" icon on the far right-hand side of your ribbon.
4. **Click** "Custom Slide Size."
5. **Click** the down arrow next to "Slides sized for:"
6. **Click** the "Banner" option.
7. **Click** OK.

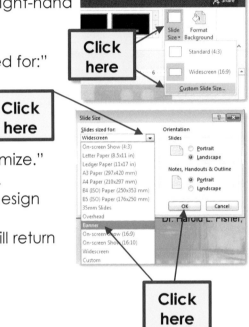

8. Another window will open. Select "Maximize."
9. **Notice** that your slides are now banners.
10. At this point you can select a different design background if necessary.
11. **Click** the undo button and your slides will return to the defaulted size.

12. **Save** and close the presentation.

Chapter 6: Glossary

Slide sorter: The slide sorter view helps you to easily rearrange the slides of your presentation.

Slide master: The slide master view allows you to control the look of your PowerPoint presentations.

Slide numbers: Slide numbers can help you as the speaker keep track of the correct slide that is being displayed that should correspond with your personal notes as well as the handouts you provide for your audience.

Chapter 6: Applying your skills

1. **Open** Microsoft PowerPoint 2016 to a new blank presentation.
2. **Add** two more slides and type Banners as the title on slide 2 and Slide numbers as the title on slide three.
3. **Rearrange** the slides so that slide 3 becomes slide two.
4. **Insert** slide numbers on all three slides.
5. **Create** a banner and add a design to the background of all three slides.

Chapter 6: Self-Assessment

1. **True or False:** Slides can be sorted in the normal view of your presentation.
2. **True or False:** The slide master is limited to changing the fonts and themes.
3. **True or False:** Slide numbers can be inserted on all slides of your presentation.
4. **True or False:** The banner option is available under the slide size icon.

Answers:

1. True
2. False (Slide master provides options to change themes, colors, fonts, effects, and background styles).
3. True
4. True

Chapter 7: Microsoft PowerPoint 2016 Creating Videos and Other Effects

✓ Saving PowerPoint as video
✓ Embedding video

✓ Saving slides as pdf/jpeg
✓ Mouse over effect

Saving PowerPoint as video

In the event you are a business owner and you want to present your PowerPoint with quality, you can save your presentation on a CD, DVD, or the internet and play it as a video. Saving it as a video is also beneficial when you send the file to someone who does not have PowerPoint on their computer.

1. **Open** the PowerPoint presentation from the last chapter.
2. **Click** on the file tab.
3. **Click** on "Export."
4. **Click** "Create a Video."
5. **Notice** the options under "Create a Video" in the middle of your window. You can choose to keep the video quality high, or click the drop down menu and change it. You can also change the recorded timings, however, you will learn how to record your timings in chapter 10 of this book. You can also change the number of seconds each slide will display in the video.

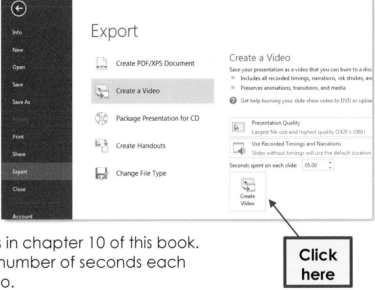

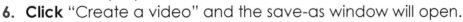

6. **Click** "Create a video" and the save-as window will open.

7. **Change** the location and name of the video file, and click save.
8. **Locate** your file and double-click on it to view the video.
9. PowerPoint video files can be saved to CDs.
10. **Click** the file tab.
11. **Click** on "Export."

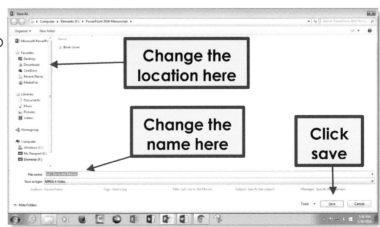

Change the location here

Change the name here

Click save

12. **Notice** the option to "Package Presentation for CD."
13. **Click** on it, then **click** "Package for CD" in the middle of your window.

    Note: Keep in mind that you will need to have a CD loaded in your CD drive on your computer in order to perform these actions.

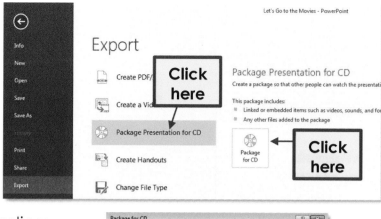

14. When you click on "Package for CD" the "Package for CD" window will open.
15. Again, the CD must already be in the drive of your computer.
16. At this point you would click "Copy to CD."
17. **Keep** your presentation open for the next section.

Embedding video

If the video (or any video) of your PowerPoint presentation has been placed on YouTube, you can embed a video from a website such as YouTube.

1. **Open** the PowerPoint presentation from the last section.
2. **Click** on slide 2 and add a new slide.
3. **Type** the words "Short Movie Clip" for the title.
4. **Click** in the "insert video" icon located in the placeholder. (Also found under the insert tab).
5. The "insert video" window will open.
6. **Type** in the "Search YouTube" area the words **"Remember the Titans"** and press the enter key on your keyboard.
7. **Select** any video and click insert. You can resize the video similar to resizing a picture. (Review chapter 3).

8. If you want to link a video at a certain starting point, **open** your internet browser (Firefox or Google Chrome) and navigate to Youtube.com.
9. **Type** in the search box "Remember the Titans: Leave no doubt."
10. **Click** on the video in the list.

11. **Look** for the word "Share" near the bottom of the video.

12. **Notice** the "Start at" option. For this example, change the "Start at" point of this video to 00.59 seconds.

13. **Copy** the link just above "Start at."

14. Go back to your PowerPoint presentation and **paste** the link on slide three.

15. **Press** the enter key on your keyboard.

16. **Click** on the "Slide Show" icon on the bottom right-hand corner of your window.

17. **Click** on the link and the internet will open and play the video at the starting point (00.59 seconds) you selected.

18. **Save** and close the presentation.

Saving slides as pdf

The acronym pdf means "portable document format." This means anyone can view the document even if they don't have any software application (such as PowerPoint) on their computer. Another reason to save your presentations as a pdf is to protect the document from unauthorized changes.

1. **Open** the PowerPoint presentation from the last section.
2. **Click** on the file tab.
3. **Click** on the "Save As" option and the "Save As" section will open in the middle of your screen.
4. **Click** "Browse" and a window will open.
5. **Change** the location to the desktop.
6. **Click** to the right of "Save as type" and in the drop-down select "PDF."
7. **Click** "Save."
8. The PDF document of your presentation should open.
9. If the document does not open, look on your desktop and **double-click** on the PDF "Let's Go to the Movies."
10. **Close** the PDF and your presentation.

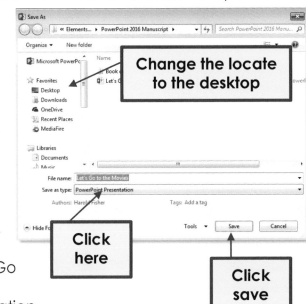

Applying mouse-over effect

The mouse-over effect allows you to simply move your cursor over an object or text and move to another hyperlinked slide without clicking on it. This is similar to the pop-up effect you have probably seen on the internet.

1. **Open** Microsoft PowerPoint 2016 to a new blank presentation.
2. **Change** your layout to "blank layout." (Review chapter 2).
3. **Add** three different shapes, a square, circle, and triangle.
4. **Click** the "insert" tab and click the "Shapes" icon.
5. **Move** your cursor over the rectangle and click once.
6. **Notice** your cursor turns into a plus sign.
7. **Click/hold/drag** your cursor and **draw** a square on your slide.
8. **Click** the insert tab, then click on the "Shapes" icon and locate the triangle and **click** on it.
9. **Draw** a triangle on your slide.
10. **Click** the insert tab, then click on the "Shapes" icon and locate the oval (circle) and **click** on it.
11. **Draw** a circle on your slide.
12. **Now** your slide should look like the example to the right.
13. **Click** on your triangle, then **right-click** and **select** "edit text."
14. **Type** the word "triangle."
15. **Repeat** steps 13 & 14 for the circle and square.
16. **Add** three blank slides.
17. **Click** on slide one.
18. **Click** on the triangle and click the insert tab.
19. **Click** on the "Action" icon.
20. The action settings window will open.
21. **Click** on the "Mouse-over" tab.
22. **Click** in the small circle next to "hyperlink to:"
23. **Click** the down arrow and select "slide."
24. The "hyperlink to slide" window will open.
25. **Click** "2. Slide 2" in the window.
26. **Click** OK.
27. **Click** OK again.
28. **Click** on your circle and **click** the insert tab. (You should still be on slide one).
29. **Click** on the "Action" icon.

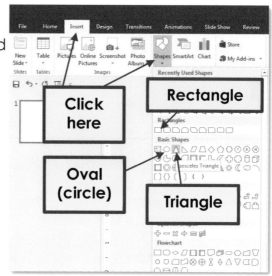

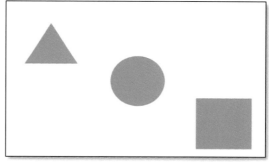

30. The action settings window will open.
31. **Click** on the "Mouse-over" tab.
32. **Click** in the small circle next to "hyperlink to:"
33. **Click** the down arrow and select "slide."
34. The "hyperlink to slide" window will open.
35. **Click** "3. Slide 3" in the window.
36. **Click** OK.
37. **Click** OK again.
38. **Click** on your square and **click** the insert tab. (You should still be on slide one).
39. **Click** on the "Action" icon.
40. The action settings window will open.
41. **Click** on the "Mouse-over" tab.
42. **Click** in the small circle next to "hyperlink to:"
43. **Click** the down arrow and select "slide."
44. The "hyperlink to slide" window will open.
45. **Click** "4. Slide 4" in the window.
46. **Click** OK.
47. **Click** OK again.
48. **Delete** slides 2, 3, & 4. (**Click** on slide 2 in the navigation window and press delete on your keyboard. Repeat the same steps for the other two slides).
49. **Right-click** on slide one in your slide navigation window and select copy in the drop-down menu.
50. **Right-click** below slide one in the navigation window and **paste** three times.
51. Your navigation slide window should look like the example to the right.
52. **Click** on slide two.
53. **Click** on your triangle.
54. **Click** on the format tab and locate the "Shape fill" icon.
55. **Click** on it and click on yellow.
56. **Repeat** the same steps for the other two shapes using the same color.
57. **Move** to slide three and change the shape colors to gold.
58. **Move** to slide four and change the shape colors to green.
59. **Click** on the "Slide Show" icon in the bottom right-hand corner of your window.
60. **Slowly** move your cursor over each shape and notice how PowerPoint will automatically move to the different slides with different colors.
61. **Close** the presentation without saving it.

Chapter 7: Glossary

Embedding video: Embedding video simply means inserting a video within your PowerPoint presentation, which makes it more engaging for your audience.

PDF: The acronym pdf means "portable document format." This means anyone can view the document even if they don't have any software application (such as PowerPoint) on their computer.

Mouse over effect: The mouse-over effect allows you to simply move your cursor over an object or text and move to another hyperlinked slide without clicking on it.

Chapter 7: Applying your skills

1. **Open** Microsoft PowerPoint 2016 to a new blank presentation and add a second slide.
2. **Locate** any YouTube video and embed into slide two.
3. **Delete** the video and **add** two different shapes on slide two and provide names on each shape.
4. **Apply** the mouse over effect to these shapes.

Chapter 7: Self-Assessment

1. **True or False:** You can change the number of seconds each slide will displayed when you are saving your presentation as a video file.
2. **True or False:** The "insert video" icon can also be found under the insert tab on your ribbon.
3. **True or False:** Another reason to save your presentations as a pdf is to allow others to make changes.
4. **True or False:** The mouse-over effect allows you to simply click on an object or text and move to another hyperlinked slide.
5. **True or False:** It is very easy to print out a document that has page border applied to it.

Answers:

1. True
2. True
3. False (Another reason to save your presentations as a pdf is to protect the document from unauthorized changes).
4. False (The mouse-over effect allows you to simply move your cursor over an object or text and move to another hyperlinked slide without clicking on it).

Chapter 8: Microsoft PowerPoint 2016
Action Buttons and Shapes

✓ Mouse click with text
✓ Action buttons

✓ Formatting shapes
✓ Mouse over with shapes

Mouse click with text

The mouse click effect is similar to navigation menus found on the internet. Similar to the way online hyperlinks help you move from one webpage to another, action settings work the same way. They allow you to move quickly around your presentation at the click of a mouse.

1. **Open** Microsoft PowerPoint to a new blank presentation.
2. **Add** two slides and **click** on slide two.
3. Let's say you wanted to create a multiple choice game. Slide two will have the question on it and slide three will display the answer.
4. **Type** the following information on slide two like the example below:
5. **Click** on slide 3 and make the title "The correct answer is:"
6. **Type**: 5,280 ft.

   Note: The text size in this case is 60 pts.

7. **Click** on slide two.
8. **Highlight** all three answers.
9. **Click** on the insert tab.
10. **Click** on the "Action" icon.
11. **Click** on "Hyperlink to:"
12. **Click** OK.
13. **Click** on the "Slide Show" icon on the bottom right-hand corner.
14. **Click** on any answer and notice that you are automatically moved to the next slide.

   Note: You can add a 4th slide that says "incorrect: try again!" In other words, if your audience selects to incorrect answer this slide will appear. Always make sure you link the correct answer to the correct slide number.

15. **Save** this presentation as "Mouse click" and **keep** the presentation open for the next section.

How many feet are in a mile?

• 5,290 ft
• 5,789 ft
• 5,280 ft.

Action buttons

Action buttons are similar to the mouse click effect. These buttons allow you to move quickly around your presentation as well.

1. **Open** the previous presentation called "Mouse click."
2. **Click** on slide 3 and add a 4th slide.
3. **Type** the following information to the right:
4. **Click** the "insert" tab.
5. **Click** the "Shapes" icon.
6. **Scroll** down to the bottom of the list under "Action buttons" and click on the "Back to Previous" button.
7. **Draw** the button in the middle of slide four.
8. The "Action Settings" window will open.
9. **Click** the "down arrow" and select "Slide"
10. The "Hyperlink to Slide" window will open.
11. **Click** on **2** in the "Slide Title" window.
12. **Click** OK.
13. **Click** OK again.
14. **Click** on the "Slide Show" icon at the bottom right-hand side of your page.
15. **Click** the "Back" button and notice that you are automatically moved to slide two where your question is located.
16. **Close** the presentation without saving it.

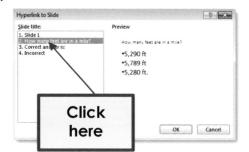

Formatting shapes

1. **Open** MS PowerPoint to a new blank presentation.
2. **Change** your slide layout to blank.
3. **Click** on the insert tab.
4. **Click** on the "Shapes" icon and draw a circle. (Review chapter 8).
5. **Notice** the "Drawing Tools: Format tab" appears.
6. **Click** on the "Shape Fill" icon and change the color to blue.
7. **Click** the "Shape Outline" icon and change the color to yellow.

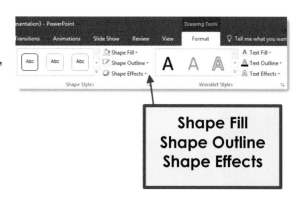

8. **Click** on the "Shape Effects" icon, move over the "Preset" option and select "Preset 4."
9. **Notice** the changes made to your shape.

10. **Close** the presentation without saving it.

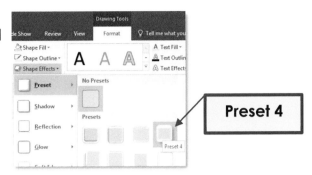

Mouse over with shapes

The mouse over effect allows you to simply click on an object or text and move to another hyperlinked slide. This is similar to the mouse over effect you learned in chapter seven.

1. **Open** Microsoft PowerPoint 2016 to a new blank presentation.
2. **Change** your layout to "blank layout." (Review chapter 2).
3. **Add** three different shapes, a square, circle, and triangle.

4. **Click** the "insert" tab and click the
5. "Shapes" icon.
6. **Move** your cursor over the rectangle and click once.
7. **Notice** your cursor turns into a plus sign.
8. **Click/hold/drag** your cursor and **draw** a square on your slide.
9. **Click** the insert tab, then click on the
10. "Shapes" icon and locate the triangle and **click** on it.
11. **Draw** a triangle on your slide.
12. **Click** the insert tab, then click on the
13. "Shapes" icon and locate the oval (circle) and **click** on it.
14. **Draw** a circle on your slide.
15. **Now** your slide should look like the example to the right.
16. **Click** on your triangle, then **right-click** and **select** "edit text."
17. **Type** the word "triangle."
18. **Repeat** steps 13 & 14 for the circle and square.
19. **Add** three blank slides.
20. **Click** on slide one.
21. **Click** on the triangle and click the insert tab.
22. **Click** on the "Action" icon.

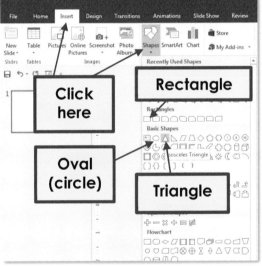

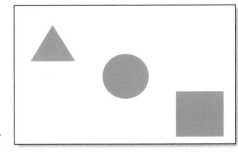

23. The action settings window will open.
24. **Click** on the "Mouse-over" tab.
25. **Click** in the small circle next to "hyperlink to:"
26. **Click** the down arrow and select "slide."
27. The "hyperlink to slide" window will open.
28. **Click** "2. Slide 2" in the window.
29. **Click** OK.
30. **Click** OK again.

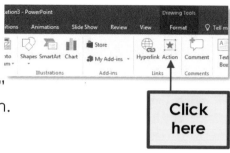

31. **Click** on your circle and **click** the insert tab. (You should still be on slide one).
32. **Click** on the "Action" icon.
33. The action settings window will open.
34. **Click** on the "Mouse-over" tab.
35. **Click** in the small circle next to "hyperlink to:"
36. **Click** the down arrow and select "slide."
37. The "hyperlink to slide" window will open.
38. **Click** "3. Slide 3" in the window.
39. **Click** OK.
40. **Click** OK again.

41. **Click** on your square and **click** the insert tab.
42. (You should still be on slide one).
43. **Click** on the "Action" icon.
44. The action settings window will open.
45. **Click** on the "Mouse-over" tab.
46. **Click** in the small circle next to "hyperlink to:"
47. **Click** the down arrow and select "slide."
48. The "hyperlink to slide" window will open.
49. **Click** "4. Slide 4" in the window.
50. **Click** OK.
51. **Click** OK again.
52. **Delete** slides 2, 3, & 4. (**Click** on slide 2 in the navigation window and press delete on your keyboard. Repeat the same steps for the other two slides).
53. **Right-click** on slide one in your slide navigation window and select copy in the drop-down menu.
54. **Right-click** below slide one in the navigation window and **paste** three times.
55. Your navigation slide window should look like the example to the right.
56. **Click** on slide two.
57. **Click** on your triangle.
58. **Click** on the format tab and locate the "Shape fill" icon.

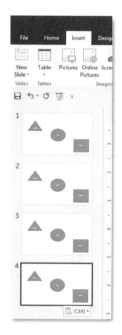

59. **Click** on it and click on yellow.
60. **Repeat** the same steps for the other two shapes using the same color.
61. **Move** to slide three and change the shape colors to gold.
62. **Move** to slide four and change the shape colors to green.

63. **Click** on the "Slide Show" icon in the bottom right-hand corner of your window.
64. **Slowly** move your cursor over each shape and notice how PowerPoint will automatically move to the different slides with different colors.
65. **Close** the presentation without saving it.

Chapter 8: Glossary

Hyperlinks: A hyperlink is a link within a document, webpage, or PowerPoint presentation that is connected to another location, which is normally activated by clicking on a highlighted word or shape.

Mouse click effect: The mouse click effect is similar to navigation menus found on the internet. Similar to the way online hyperlinks help you move from one webpage to another, action settings work the same way. They allow you to move quickly around your presentation at the click of a mouse.

Mouse over effect: The mouse over effect allows you to simply click on an object or text and move to another hyperlinked slide.

Chapter 8: Applying your skills

1. **Open** Microsoft PowerPoint 2016 to a new blank presentation.
2. **Add** three slides.
3. **Type** the following question within the title of slide 2: What is the tab location of action buttons?
4. **Type** the following answers below the title on slide 2: Under the Slide Show tab, Under the insert tab.
5. **Click** on slide 3 and type the word "Correct" in the title. Below the title type "The correct answer is: Under the insert tab."
6. **Apply** the mouse click effect to your answers on slide two to connect with slide three.

Chapter 8: Self-Assessment

1. **True or False:** Mouse click and mouse over effects both include hyperlinks.
2. **True or False:** Action buttons are similar to creating a webpage.
3. **True or False:** The action buttons are found under the "Shapes" icon.
4. **True or False:** The shape fill icon helps when you want to add outline color.

Answers:

1. True
2. False (Action buttons are similar to the mouse click effect. These buttons allow you to move quickly around your presentation as well).
3. True
4. True
5. False (The shape fill icon helps when you want to add color to an object).

Chapter 9: Microsoft PowerPoint 2016
Adding Tables and Charts

✓ Adding a table
✓ Formatting a table

✓ Adding a chart
✓ Formatting a chart

Adding a table

Tables help you to organize your text and data within your presentations.

1. **Open** MS PowerPoint to a new blank presentation.
2. **Add** a second slide.
3. **Click** on the insert table icon located in the middle of your slide.
4. The "Insert Table" window will open.
5. **Add** six columns and four rows.
6. **Click** OK.
7. Your table will appear on the slide.

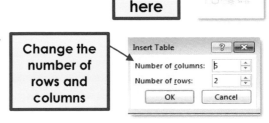

8. **Type** the following information within your table. (**Note**: Simply click within each cell to type the information or you can use your "tab" key on your keyboard to move from one cell to the next).

FirstName	LastName	Address	City	State	Zip
John	Daring	12980 1st St.	Houston	Texas	77002
Jacob	Trickster	1234 2nd St.	Spring	Texas	77379
Moses	Mumbler	6745 3rd St.	Houston	Texas	77005

9. **Save** this presentation as "Table" and **keep** it open for the next section.

Formatting a table

1. **Open** the "Table" presentation from the last section.
2. **Click** on slide two where your table is located.
3. **Click** inside any cell in the table you just created from the previous lesson.
4. **Notice** the "**design**" tab that appears on the ribbon. (Under table tools).
5. **Click** on the "design tab.

6. **Click** the "down-arrow" at the end of the "table styles" section of the ribbon.
7. Slowly move your cursor over each table style.

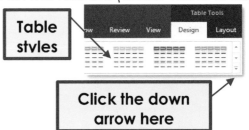

8. **Search** for the "**Grid Table 4 – Accent 4**" style and **click** on it.
9. Your table should look like the example below.

First Name	Last Name	Address	City	State	Zip
John	Daring	12980 1st St.	Houston	Texas	77002
Jacob	Trickster	1234 2nd St.	Spring	Texas	77379
Moses	Mumbler	6745 3rd St.	Houston	Texas	77005

10. We can also add more columns and rows to our table if necessary.
11. **Click** inside the cell where the zip code of 77005 is found.
12. **Click** on the "Layout" tab.
13. **Click** on the "**Insert below**" option.
14. A new row will be added.

15. **Click** in the last row, and click "Insert Right.
16. **Notice** a new column has been added.

Note: Columns run down the table and rows are across a table.

17. **Place** your cursor within the top cell to the right of "Zip."
18. **Insert** a row above."
19. **Type "Addresses"** in the first cell above "First Name."
20. **Highlight** all of the cells in this new row by **holding** on to your cursor (left-click) in the first cell above "First Name" and moving it over to the right until you reach the last column. All of the cells in the first row should be highlighted.
21. **Click** the "**Layout tab**" on your ribbon under "Table tools."

22. **Click** "**Merge Cells**."
23. **Click** on your Home tab and click the "**Center**" command.

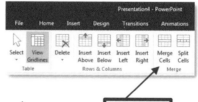

24. Your table should look like the following example.

Addresses						
FirstName	LastName	Address	City	State	Zip	
John	Daring	12980 1st St.	Houston	Texas	77002	
Jacob	Trickster	1234 2nd St.	Spring	Texas	77379	
Moses	Mumbler	6745 3rd St.	Houston	Texas	77005	

25. **Keep** the presentation open for the next section.

Adding a chart

Charts make it easier to spot trends, make comparisons and contrast within your data by inserting a bar, area, or line chart.

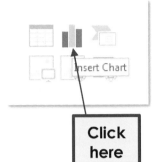

1. **Open** the presentation from the last section.
2. **Click** on slide 2 of your presentation.
3. **Add** another slide.
4. **Click** on the "insert chart" icon in the middle of your slide.
5. The "Insert Chart" window will open.
6. **Click** OK.
7. A chart will be inserted into your slide and a data sheet with text and numbers will open so that you can make necessary changes.
8. **Save** and **keep** the presentation open for the next section.

Formatting a chart

1. **Open** the presentation from the last section.
2. **Click** on slide 3 of your presentation.

   Note: You may need to click on top of your chart and then click on the design tab.

3. **Notice** the options on your ribbon under the design tab.

4. **Click** on the "Change Colors" icon and **move** your cursor over each color. Notice how there is a preview provided as you move over each color.
5. **Select** any color pattern.
6. **Notice** the "Chart Styles" section.
7. **Click** on the down arrow at the end of the chart styles section.
8. **Select** any chart style option.
9. **Notice** the "Change Chart Type" icon on the far right-hand side of the ribbon.

10. **Click** on it and the "Change Chart Type" window will open.
11. **Click** on the "Pie" option.
12. **Click** OK.
13. Now your chart is a pie chart.
14. **Close** the presentation without saving it.

Chapter 9: Glossary

Merge cells: Merge cells means to combine a selected number of cells into one cell.

Charts: Charts make it easier to spot trends, make comparisons and contrast within your data by inserting a bar, area, or line chart.

Tables: Tables help you to organize your text and data within your presentations.

Chapter 9: Applying your skills

1. **Open** Microsoft PowerPoint 2016 to a new blank document.
2. **Add** two slides and click on slide two.
3. **Insert** a table with 3 columns and 4 rows.
4. **Format** the table by applying any design.
5. **Insert** a pie chart on slide three.

Chapter 9: Self-Assessment

1. **True or False:** You can use your "tab" key on your keyboard to move from one cell to the next in a table.
2. **True or False:** The insert table command is found under the design tab.
3. **True or False:** You can add a row to an existing table.
4. **True or False:** The merge cells command is located under the "Table Tools Design" tab.
5. **True or False:** You can still change the chart type after you have already created a chart.

Answers:
1. True
2. False (The insert table command is found either on your slide or under the insert tab).
3. True
4. False (The merge cells command is located under the layout tab).
5. True

Chapter 10: Microsoft PowerPoint 2016 Customizing and Adding Voice Over

✓ Creating a custom show
✓ Rehearsing a slide show
✓ Smart Art
✓ Layering effect
✓ Adding voice over

Creating a custom show

1. **Open** MS PowerPoint to a new blank presentation.
2. **Type** "Custom Show" as the title.
3. **Add** a new slide and type "New Slide Show" in the title placeholder.
4. **Click** on the "Slide Show" tab.
5. **Click** on the "Custom Slide Show" icon.
6. **Click** "Custom Show" and a small custom show window will open.
7. **Click** the "New" icon and the "Define Custom Show" window will open.
8. **Check** in the boxes next to "Custom show" and "New Slide Show."
9. **Click** the "Add" button in the middle of your window.
10. This will move the slides over to the "Slides in custom show" side.
11. **Click** the "OK" button.
12. The "Custom Shows" button should still be open.
13. **Click** on the "Show" button and the Slide show will begin.
14. **Press** the escape key on your keyboard to exit the slide show.
15. **Close** the "Custom Shows" window.
16. **Click** the "Custom Slide Show" icon on your ribbon and notice the show you created called "Custom Show 1."

Note: You can click on "Custom Shows" again and edit the name of the show.

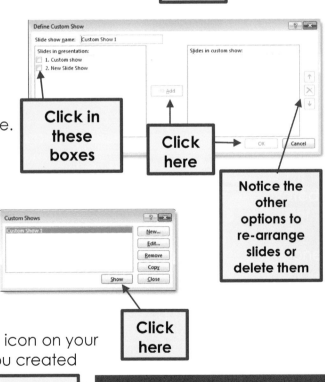

17. **Save** the presentation as "Custom Show."
18. **Keep** this presentation open for the next section.

Rehearsing a show

Rehearsing a slide show presentation is just as important as rehearsing to speak before an audience within any environment. PowerPoint allows you to rehearse your presentations and will automatically provide timings of slide advancement for each slide.

1. **Open** the presentation from the previous section.
2. **Click** on the "Slide Show" tab.
3. **Click** on the "Rehearse timings" icon.
4. You should be in "Slide Show" at this point and a timer will appear in the upper left-hand corner of your screen.
5. The arrow on the timer allows you to advance to the next slide.

6. **Click** the arrow now.
7. The two bars to the right of the arrow allow you to pause the recording of your presentation.
8. The amount of time you spent on a slide is visible.
9. The curved arrow will allow you to repeat the recording of a slide.
10. **Click** the arrow until you exit the recording and a window will appear revealing the total amount of time spent on the slide and asking you if you want to save your slide timings.
11. **Click** "Yes."
12. **Click** the "Slide Show" tab and click "From Beginning."
13. **Notice** that your slide show will automatically advance to the end of the show.
14. **Close** the presentation without saving it.

Smart Art

SmartArt can be used to visually communicate information through different graphical layouts. SmartArt can also be found in Word, Excel and PowerPoint 2016.

1. **Open** PowerPoint 2016 to a new blank presentation.
2. **Add** a second blank slide.
3. **Click** on the "Insert" tab.
4. **Click** the "SmartArt" icon.
5. The "Choose a Smart Art Graphic" window will open.

6. **Notice** the options you have within the SmartArt window.

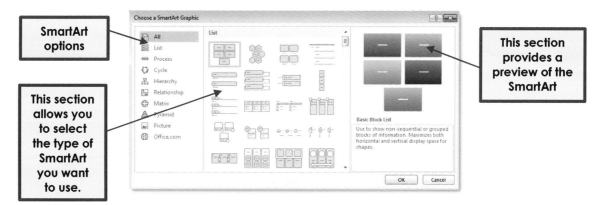

7. For this lesson you will practice SmartArt using the hierarchy layout.
8. **Click** the "Hierarchy" option on the left-hand side.

9. **Click** the first option "Organizational Chart" and **click** the **OK** button.

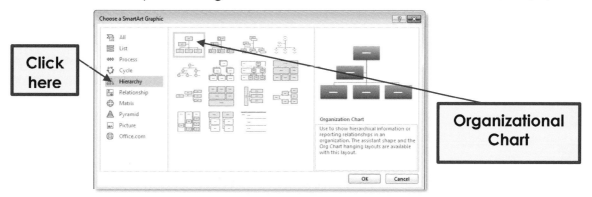

10. The chart will appear within your blank document.

11. **Notice** the example of the SmartArt on the next page.

12. **Notice** the word [Text] on the left side of the window and within the chart.
13. You can type our text in either section by simply clicking once and typing.
14. **Type** "President" in the first box at the top.
15. **Type** "Vice President" in the next box below.
16. In the three boxes below **type** Executive 1, Executive 2, and Executive 3.
17. You can resize these boxes if necessary just like the example of resizing under the "cropping" section in this chapter (steps 25-29).
18. You can add color similar to the previous shapes lesson, steps 9-13.

19. Your SmartArt Hierarchy should look like the example below.

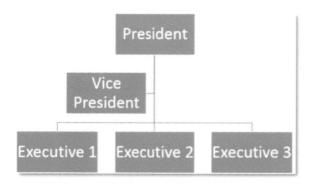

20. You can also add or delete a shape within this hierarchy.
21. **Click** on "Executive 3" and press the delete key on your keyboard.
22. **Click** the "undo" button on your quick-access toolbar.
23. **Place** your cursor behind "Executive 3" in the navigation box on the left-hand side.

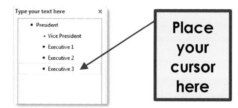

24. **Press** the "Enter" key on your keyboard.
25. **Notice** another rectangle was added to your chart.
26. **Place** your cursor at the end of "Vice President" in this same window.
27. **Press** the "Enter" key on your keyboard.
28. **Notice** another rectangle was added to your chart.
29. Your chart should look like the example below.

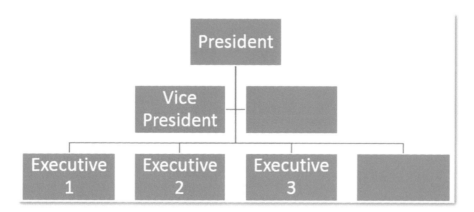

30. **Close** the presentation without saving it.

Layering effect

In this section you will learn how to create a layering effect where an object will pass through another object.

1. **Open** PowerPoint 2016 to a new blank presentation.
2. Basically, you will create an effect where the cheetah will jump through a hoop.
3. **Change** the slide layout to blank.
4. **Go** to **pixabay.com** and locate the following picture. (Search for "cheetah").
5. **Copy** and **paste** the cheetah on the left slide of your slide. **(Note:** Select the first paste option like the example to the right.)
6. **Click** the insert tab.
7. **Click** the shapes icon and locate the "Donut" shape in the menu.
8. **Draw** the donut shape on the right-hand side of your slide.
9. **Your** slide should now look like this.
10. **Notice** the small yellow dot on the inside of the donut shape.
11. **Click/hold/drag** it to the left in order to make the donut as thin (1/4 of an inch).
12. Your donut should look similar to the example to the right.
13. **Right-click** on the donut shape and select "cut" in the drop down menu.
14. **Click** the bottom part of your Paste button and click "Paste Special."
15. The "Paste Special" window will open.
16. **Select** "Picture PNG" and click OK.
17. The donut shape will appear on your slide.
18. **Right-click** on the shape and select "copy" from the drop down menu.
19. **Click** on the "Picture tools Format" tab.
20. **Click** on the top part of the "Crop" icon.
21. **Move** your cursor over the black bar on the right-hand side of your donut.
22. **Click/hold/drag** to the left until half of the donut shape is cut off.
23. **Click** anywhere on your slide and notice half of the donut will be missing.
24. **Right-click** and paste. Another donut will appear.
25. Repeat steps 19-20.
26. **Move** your cursor over the black bar on the left-hand side of your donut.

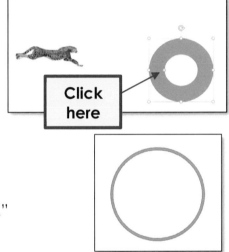

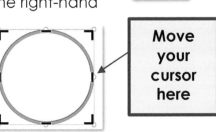

27. **Click/hold/drag** to the right until half of the donut shape is cut off.
28. **Click** anywhere on your slide.
29. **Make** sure the two sides of the donut shape are connected.
30. **Click** the right side of the shape.
31. **Click** on the "Picture tools format" tab.
32. **Click** the down arrow on the "Send Backward" icon.

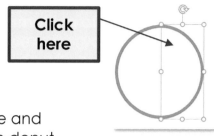

33. **Click** "Send to Back."
34. **Move** the cheetah through the donut shape and notice it will move behind the left side of the donut shape and in front of the right side.
35. **Move** the cheetah back to the left-hand side of your slide.
36. **Click** on the animations tab.
37. **Click** the down arrow for "More" animations.
38. **Click** on "More Motion paths" near the bottom of the list.
39. The "Change Motion Path" window will open.
40. **Locate** "More" and click on it.
41. **Click** OK.

42. **Move** your cursor over the edge of the dot at the end of the line and it will turn into a double-sided arrow.
43. **Click/hold/drag** the line past the right side of the slide.
44. **Click** on the "Slide Show" icon on the bottom right-hand side of your window.
45. **Press** your space bar and notice the cheetah will move behind the left side of the donut shape and in front of the right side.
46. **Close** the presentation without saving it.

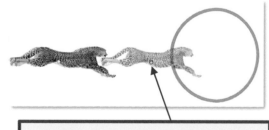

Place your cursor here and look for a double-sided arrow. Click/hold/drag it past the right side of your slide.

Adding voice over

Voice over in PowerPoint allows you to record your voice for each slide. For example, if you wanted to do a quick lecture for your presentation and send it to someone, you can create a presentation that includes your audio. The voice over option is similar to rehearsing a show. Also, most laptops have built-in microphones to accomplish this task.

Note: If you are using a desktop computer for this section you will need an external microphone.

1. **Open** the presentation called "Let's Go to the Movies."
2. In the event you don't have this presentation, create the following slides:

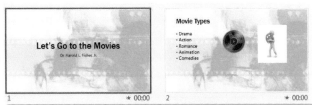

3. **Click** the "Slide Show" tab.
4. **Click** on "Record Slide Show."

5. **Notice** the two options: "Start Recording from the Beginning" or "Start Recording from the Current Slide."
6. **Click** on "Start Recording from the Beginning."
7. The "Record Slide Show" window will open.
8. **Click** "Start Recording."
9. You will be in slide show and the "Recording" icon will appear in the upper left-hand corner of your screen.
15. You should be in "Slide Show" at this point and a timer will appear in the upper left-hand corner of your screen.

16. The arrow on the timer allows you to advance to the next slide.
17. **Click** the arrow now.
18. The two bars to the right of the arrow allow you to pause the recording of your presentation.
19. The amount of time you spent on a slide is visible.
20. The curved arrow will allow you to repeat the recording of a slide.
21. **Click** the arrow until you exit the recording and a window will appear revealing the total amount of time spent on the slide and asking you if you want to save your slide timings.
22. **Click** "Yes."
23. **Click** the "Slide Show" tab and click "From Beginning."
24. **Notice** that your slide show will automatically advance to the end of the show.
25. **Close** the document without saving it.

Chapter 10: Glossary

SmartArt: SmartArt can be used to visually communicate information through different graphical layouts.

Paste Special: Paste special allows you to specify formatting of objects, text, and pictures from other programs or from a particular slide within your presentation.

Voice over: Voice over in PowerPoint allows you to record your voice for each slide.

Chapter 10: Applying your skills

1. **Open** Microsoft PowerPoint 2016 to a new blank document.
2. **Add** a second slide with text and pictures and create a custom show.
3. **Create** layering effect with a lion jumping through a circle.
4. **Add** voice over to this presentation.

Chapter 10: Self-Assessment

1. **True or False:** After you click on custom slide show, you will need to click on the "custom presentation" icon.
2. **True or False**: Rehearsing a presentation is critical to the success of a presentation.
3. **True or False:** One of the icons used when creating a layering effect is "Send Backwards."
4. **True or False:** Most desktops have built-in microphones.
5. **True or False:** The Smart Art command is located under the "Smart Art" tab.

Answers:

1. False (You will click on "Custom Show.")
2. True
3. True
4. False (Laptops have built-in microphones).
5. False (Smart Art is located under the insert tab)

Glossary

Animation: These are the effects that set up the way you want text, picture, or an object to appear on your slide during a slide show presentation.

Bullets: The purpose of bullets is to make key points. Bullets are used in MS Word as well as MS PowerPoint.

Charts: Charts make it easier to spot trends, make comparisons and contrast within your data by inserting a bar, area, or line chart.

Cut command: The cut command will move text, pictures, and objects to a different location.

Design themes: These options make it much easier to coordinate the colors of your background and text for your presentation. They are preformatted backgrounds that you can apply instead of manually changing the text colors and backgrounds.

Duration: The amount of time the transition will take place when your presentation advances to the next slide.

Embedding video: Embedding video simply means inserting a video within your PowerPoint presentation, which makes it more engaging for your audience.

Gradient fill: This option provides a gradual blending to two or more colors within a shape or the background of a slide.

Gridlines: Gridlines help you to align your pictures and objects on a slide.

Hyperlinks: A hyperlink is a link within a document, webpage, or PowerPoint presentation that is connected to another location, which is normally activated by clicking on a highlighted word or shape.

Merge cells: Merge cells means to combine a selected number of cells into one cell.

Mouse click effect: The mouse click effect is similar to navigation menus found on the internet. Similar to the way online hyperlinks help you move from one webpage to another, action settings work the same way. They allow you to move quickly around your presentation at the click of a mouse.

Mouse over effect: The mouse over effect allows you to simply click on an object or text and move to another hyperlinked slide.

Mouse over effect: The mouse-over effect allows you to simply move your cursor over an object or text and move to another hyperlinked slide without clicking on it.

Paste Special: Paste special allows you to specify formatting of objects, text, and pictures from other programs or from a particular slide within your presentation.

PDF: The acronym pdf means "portable document format." This means anyone can view the document even if they don't have any software application (such as PowerPoint) on their computer.

Placeholder: The placeholders are the dotted borders of text boxes found within different slide layouts. They help to guide the users in the placement of titles and bullet points.

Ribbon: This is the menu bar and tabs located at the top of your PowerPoint software. It contains several different commands used to create a presentation.

Slide master: The slide master view allows you to control the look of your PowerPoint presentations.

Slide numbers: Slide numbers can help you as the speaker keep track of the correct slide that is being displayed that should correspond with your personal notes as well as the handouts you provide for your audience.

Slide show view: This is the view you will be using to display your presentation before an audience.

Slide show: A slide show is a collection of slides arranged in a certain order that contain text, images, and objects for presenting before an audience.

Slide sorter: The slide sorter view helps you to easily rearrange the slides of your presentation.

SmartArt: SmartArt can be used to visually communicate information through different graphical layouts.

Speaker notes: The purpose of speaker notes is for you to use as a reference while you are presenting your PowerPoint presentation to an audience.

Tables: Tables help you to organize your text and data within your presentations.

Transition: Slide transitions are visual movements that occur between slides. For example, when you move from one slide to the next, you can apply any type of slide transition

Transparency: This is the setting in PowerPoint that allows you to change a picture from a darker color to a brighter contrast.

Undo and re-do: The undo command will reverse the previous actions performed in a document or multiple actions that occurred previously. The redo command will repeat the last action. However, once you save and close a document you cannot undo or redo previous actions when you open the document again.

Voice over: Voice over in PowerPoint allows you to record your voice for each slide.

Sources

All screenshots "Used with permission from Microsoft Corporation."

Abu-Jabar, M. (2016). Thirty interesting facts you may not know about computers and the Internet. Retrieved from http://thefuturetech.com/2013/04/06/30-interesting-facts-about-computers-internet/

Brown, K. (2016). A Terabyte of Storage Space. How much is too much. Retrieved from http://aimblog.uoregon.edu/2014/07/08/a-terabyte-of-storage-space-how-much-is-too-much/#.VpsHLFLiDcc

Churches, A., (2008). Bloom's Taxonomy Blooms Digitally. Retrieved from http://teachnology.pbworks.com/f/Bloom%5C%27s+Taxonomy+Blooms+Digitally.pdf

Colmer, R. S. (2007). The senior's Guide to Easy Computing-Updated! Chelsea, MI: Eklektika Press.

Cox, J. and Lambert, J. (2010). Windows 7 Step by Step. Redmond, WA: Microsoft Press.

Defeo, J. (2005). Portable Storage Devices. PC Mag article. Retrieved from http://www.pcmag.com/article2/0,2817,1789743,00.asp

Definitions in the basic computer vocabulary were retrieved from http://www.webopedia.com

Deleon, R. (2002). Basic Home Networking. Clifton Park, NY: Thomson.

Excel and Access lesson ideas were retrieved from http://www.inpics.net.

Front cover and inside photo purchased and retrieved from http://www.dreamstime.com

Frye, C. D., Lambert, J., and Cox, J. (2011). Redmond, WA: Microsoft Press.

How to Geek. (2016). Ten important computer practices you should follow. Retrieved from http://www.howtogeek.com/173478/10-important-computer-security-practices-you-should-follow/

Gregory, P. H. (2011). Computer Viruses For Dummies. Hoboken, NJ: Wiley Publishing.

Gunter, S. K. (2010). Office 2010 Visual Quick Tips. Indianapolis, IN: Wiley Publishing.

Helding, L. (2011). Digital Natives and Digital Immigrants: Teaching and Learning in the Digital Age. Journal Of Singing, 68(2), 199-206.

Joyce, J. (2010). Windows 7 Plain & Simple. Redmond, WA: Microsoft Press.

Kathayat, P. (2016). Interesting, Unknown and Amazing Computer Facts. Retrieved from http://techgeekers.com/45-interesting-unknown-and-amazing-facts-about-computers/

Kraynak, J. (2011). The Complete Idiot's Guide to Computer Basics, 3E. New York, NY: Penguin Group.

Maron, R. (2010). Maran Illustrated Windows 7. Boston, MA: Maran Graphics.

Maran, R. (2010). Maran Illustrated Computers. Boston, MA: Maran Graphics.

McFedries, P. (2009). Windows 7 Simplified. Indianapolis, IN: Wiley Publishing.

McFedries, P. (2009). Teach Yourself VISUALLY Windows 7. Indianapolis, IN: Wiley Publishing.

Miller, M. (2010). Easy Computer Basics, Windows 7 Upper Saddle River, NJ: Pearson Education.

Miller, M. (2010). Absolute Beginner's Guide to Computer Basics. Upper Saddle River, NJ: Pearson Education.

Murray, K. (2010). Microsoft Office 2010 Plain & Simple. Redmond, WA: Microsoft Press.

Nikirk, M. (2009). Today's millennial generation: A look ahead to the future they create. Techniques: Connecting education and careers, 84(5), 20-23. Retrieved from ERIC database.

PC APP Spot. (2016). Twenty interesting facts about computers. Retrieved from http://www.pcappspot.com/interesting-computer-facts/

PCTools. (2016). What are crackers and hackers? Retrieved from http://www.pctools.com/security-news/crackers-and-hackers/

Pogue, D. (2003). Switching to the Mac: The Missing Manual. Pogue Press.

Prensky, M. (2001). Digital Natives Digital Immigrants. On the Horizon. MCB University Press, Vol. 9 No. 5.

Price, M. (2011). Computer Basics in Easy Steps. Southam, UK: Easy Steps Limited.

Qureshi, S., & Noteboom, C. (2006). Adaptation in distributed projects: Collaborative processes in digital natives and digital immigrants. Conference on systems sciences. IEEE Computer Society Press.

Senior Service Council. (2010). Beginning Windows 7. Retrieved from http://www.fallbrookpcusersgroup.org/Beginning_Windows_7_Lesson_4.pdf

Shelly, G. B. and Cashman, S. (2010). Discovering Computers 2011. Boston, MA: Course Technology.

Shoup, K. (2010). Teach Yourself VISUALLY Office 2010. Indianapolis, IN: Wiley Publishing.

Stokes, A. (2008). Is This Thing On?, revised edition: A Computer Handbook for Late Bloomers, Technophobes, and the Kicking & Screaming. New York, NY: Workman Publishing.

Studio Visual Steps. (2009). Windows 7 for Seniors: For Senior Citizens Who Want to Start Using Computers. Visual Steps Publishing.

Studio Visual Steps. (2009). Microsoft Office 2010 and 2007 for Seniors. Visual Steps Publishing.

Studio Visual Steps. (2009). Protect, Clean Up and Speed Up Your Computer for Seniors. Visual Steps Publishing.

Stokes, A. (2005). It's Never Too Late to Love a Computer: The Fearless Guide for Seniors. Visual Steps Publishing.

Techopedia. What is Word? Retrieved from https://www.techopedia.com/definition/3840/microsoft-word

Toly, K. (2011). Switching from PC to Mac Survival Guide: Step-by-Step User Guide for Switching to a Mac: The Basics, Managing Hardware, Managing Media, and Much More. Createspace Publishing.

Walkenbach, J., Tyson, H., Groh, M. R., Wempen, F. and Bucki, L. A. (2010). Office 2010 Bible. Indianapolis, IN: Wiley Publishing.

Wells, D. (2005). Computer Literacy BASICS: A Comprehensive Guide to IC3. Boston, MA: Course Technology.

White, R. and Downs, T. E. (2011). Introduction to Computers. Boston, MA: Course Technology.

Zeitz, L. E. (2005). Keyboarding Made Simple: Learn the best techniques for keyboarding like a pro. New York, NY: Broadway Books.

Zimmerman, L., & A. Trekles Milligan. (2007). Perspectives on communicating with the Net Generation. Innovate 4(2). Retrieved from http://www.howtogeek.com/173478/10-important-computer-security-practices-you-should-follow/

Dr. Harold L. Fisher has been a professor at College of Biblical Studies in Houston, Texas for the last eight years, and has been teaching for multiple universities online for the last nine years. Prior to becoming a professor, he taught in Galena Park and Spring Independent School Districts for a total of eight years.

He received his doctorate degree in teacher leadership from Walden University, a master's degree in education from American Intercontinental University in instructional technology, a master's degree in education from Our Lady of the Lake University with dual majors in curriculum and instruction and master technology teaching, and he completed a third master's degree in organizational leadership from Baptist Bible Seminary. He finished his Bachelors of Science degree in biblical studies from College of Biblical Studies, a teacher certification in Business Education from Texas State University, and online certification training from Lone Star College.

He was the recipient of the 2009 Teacher of the Year award in Spring I.S.D. and the 2009 Teacher of the year for the Spring I.S.D. Virtual High School, featured as the 2009 Teacher of the Month (June) by KPRC Channel 2 Houston, and in 2009 he was recognized by Harris County Region 4 as Teacher of the Year. He was nominated by his peers to receive an award to the Delta Epsilon Chi Honor Society for Biblical Higher Education for his intellectual achievement, Christian character, and leadership ability.

He is the author of five books, "Virtual Schooling through the eyes of Teachers," "Attitudes and Perspectives About Teaching of Teachers Who Provide Online Instruction at the Secondary Level," "A Technology Workbook for Adult Learners: An Introduction to Microsoft Office 2010," "A Technology Workbook for Christian Learners: Introduction to Microsoft Office 2010," and Microsoft Word 2016 Made Easy. Also, he will publish Microsoft Word, Excel, and PowerPoint 2016 for Mac users during the summer of 2016.

He has been married to his beautiful wife, Kym for twenty-two years. They have three kids, Brittani, Nicholas, and Sydnee. Dr. Fisher's favorite activities are golf, research, and spending vacation time with his wife and kids.

Search for Dr. Fisher's video tutorials at udemy.com:

Microsoft Word 2016 Made Easy
Microsoft PowerPoint 2016 Made Easy
Microsoft Excel 2016 Made Easy
Microsoft Office 2010 Made Easy

Digital books are also available at **www.redshelf.com**
Contact Dr. Fisher at drhlfisher@gmail.com

CPSIA information can be obtained
at www.ICGtesting.com
Printed in the USA
LVIC06n1254120517
534304LV00003B/12